MY GHOST AND OTHER POEMS

MY GHOST
AND OTHER
POEMS

Richard I. Gold

J2B Publishing

The information address
J2B Publishing LLC
4251 Columbia Park Road
Pomfret, MD 20657
www.J2BLLC.com
GladToDoIt@gmail.con

Cover Photo: Crater Club Clubhouse by Luke Cammack Brewster

Printed and bonded in the United States of America

ISBN: 978-1-948747-67-7

Dedication

My thanks for the support of my wife who helped me in the initial editing and my sister in law, Brenda Hurley who made valuable suggestions for some lines.

Table of Contents

INTRODUCTION

Everyone receives advice from those around them all the time. It is natural to attempt to modify the behavior and life of those around us to make a better world for all of us. Sometimes this is done in a constructive manner, sometimes in a manner that might pull us down. We should always consider the advice. If it builds us up we will be better for it. If we do not like the advice we can always choose to ignore it (which we do the vast amount of the time.)

MY GHOST

I have a ghost that walks with me
It goes where ever I go
It is the ghost of who I was
It is all I've done, all I know

When I was young and spry
The world was there for me
It was for me to use
As I went to see what I could see

But as I went and did my thing
What I did went with me
I began to realize that my plate was filling
Things were there for me to see

Now as I live, I'm not alone
Even though no one else is here
My memories are ever with me
The older I get, it is more clear

But what was done was done
There is no changing that
I must live with the younger me
The memories can leave me flat

The present is where I am
The past is what fate did give
I must prepare for the future
This is where I will live

But my ghost casts a shadow
Over all I attempt to do
For as the now is now
My ghost showed what is true

WHEN I WAS YOUNG

When I was young and full of youth
I longed for many things
Some were just and true
Some were to have the fun that pleasure brings

As I moved into the world
To make my way
I looked for whatever I wanted
At least for what I could pay

Then I married and had children
I tried to raise them as I should
They pushed, they moved into the world
The family came as they would

Now I am old and gray
I remember what ere I did
The things that passed me by
Are ghosts that do my spirit bid

For I remember what I did
It lives with me both night and day
These ghosts are ever with me
They bid me in what I do or say

Remember when you are young
You carry with you everything you do or say
Be very careful that what you create is good
When you are old your spirit will have to pay

When I was young some chose to insult me
They did not know what they should do
For what they said and what they were
Many times to themselves they were not true

For actions are remembered
Words said also do the same
For when others they need
The memories will cause a pain

THE THREE FORGIVENESS'S OF SIN

We all have sinned in who we are
Sinned of body, of soul and of mind
We can live with this if forgiven
This is for what we pine

We sin as we live our life
Not necessarily what we desire to do
We desire to live as we should
Do what is kind and just and true

By our very nature
We sin against both God and man
Our evil is with us always
We wish to be free of it, if we can

Because of who we are
We sin against God on High
He can forgive us if we truly repent
Allow us to His person draw nigh

Once God has forgiven
We must receive forgiveness from our fellow man
This forgiveness may be harder to obtain
For others know me as I truly am

Once we have forgiveness
From God and our fellow man
Comes the most difficult forgiveness of all
We must forgive ourselves, if we can

For we are part of all we've done
This is forever with us
It eats our inner self
It is something difficult to discuss

We do not truly understand
What true forgiveness doth entail
True forgiveness means to forget
To have others not to rail

Some sins can never be forgiven
By men on this earth
But forgiveness by the will of God
Involves spiritual rebirth

For the forgiveness of man
Wanting this is very well
We may wonder how to begin
However, remember "Payback is Hell"

Often we must remember
That we will have to pay
For damage done
So be careful, because there may not be a way

To forgive ourselves
Is the hardest thing we can do
What we did, what we do
So be kind, just and true

There are three forgiveness's
For the evil we did
No end of all we have
It is the end that will bid

TOMORROW

Tomorrow and tomorrow and tomorrow
We trace our path through time
From the moment we are born
Until we are beyond our prime

We live and love and do all things
That makes us who we are
Think not of what we have
But what we will become by far

Then when we reach our end
Our life's essence fully spent
We will cross the great divide
And wonder where life's time went

WHAT DO WE EXPECT?

What do we expect?
From the world where we live
Do we expect to get
Or do we expect to give

Those who expect to get
Will never have enough
When their benefactor quest
Thinking then that they have it rough

But for those who expect to give
And to get nothing in return
They see this world as an interim place
On their way to paradise for which they yearn

It is nice to get what we want
Without having to pay
But that place for most of us
Is our destiny for another day

WHAT WOULD YOU OWN?

What would you own?
That your happiness would insure
It is not the things
Or experiences that endure

The many prizes you have won
And recognitions that you crave
To know what you should
To know what you need to save

Would you own the future?
Would you make it your own?
Prepare for what may occur
For the future you prefer

THE CORRIDORS OF TIME

Whatever we decide to do
We should look down the corridors of time
For the decisions we make
Will take our future's prime

We know what the past has held
We know what the present will give
But the future is a murky field
Where we will ever live

But we must make decisions
What is the way of life
A good decision or bad
Will determine your future's strife

GLORY DAYS

These are the glory days
With the taste of honey
When things are going well
And there's plenty of money

Extend these days
From now to forever
Let the lean and lank days
Come to us never

But come they will
As surely as night follows day
Suddenly they are upon us
We can't get out of their way

But prepare we must
Else we cannot live
For when the drain opens up
No one will have ought to give

Prepare, prepare, prepare
We must be persistent
For when there is nothing else
It'll assure our existence

TODAY IS THURSDAY

Today is Thursday
One more day to work
So much to do
Our duty we dare not shirk

The weekend
The glorious weekend
We enjoy the break
Then we begin again

Work seems a cycle
Never quite the same
We try to get ahead
Our bills to tame

But to work with adeptness
Satisfaction and pride
We must do our best
From responsibility we cannot hide

A TIME TO STUDY

A time to study
A test to come
Things to know
Life's race to run

Know it all
We cannot do
For forever and a day
They come up with things anew

Prepare for the future
The past we now know
The present is building
The future you have to sow

A SPOT IN TIME

A spot in time
Take an idea for a walk
No telling where it'll lead
Then people will talk

A touch of class
A humble way
If you go wrong
You'll have to pay

A little wealth
Makes the economy strong
Excessive wealth
You may go wrong

OUR REASON FOR BEING

Our reason for being
Is one we should never have to give
For being is being
As through life we live

The reason for our being
Is not a question asked
But a statement of fact
As we undertake life's tasks

So live life each day
Give to life your all
So that when others ask
Your existence will not fall

WALK THE TIGHT ROPE

Walk the tight rope
Over the chasm of life
Your balance must be just so
Don't cut the rope with a knife

You think there are forces
Winds of change blow
Can upset your balance
Sending you down below

Stay the course
Hold with a steady hand
We're sailing into the future
To look for our promised land

DAYS AND NIGHTS

Days and nights
Nights and days
The morning sun
Burns off the haze

Birds sing
In the trees
All is well
Life's a breeze

Then it hits
From the sky
The asteroid comes
Death draws nigh

Suddenly everything changes
From pleasant to rain
What we thought desirable
Now is no gain

So look to the sky
Look out and see
For what we know not
Could easily come to be

GREET EACH DAY

Greet each day with a smile
Grant an audience to each minute
Live life to the fullest
For your own self is in it

Give to those in need
Offer yourself as a gift
For in giving what they need
You give your life a lift

Know this always
You are loved by what you give
You will be remembered
This is how you lived

THE DAY OF MAN

The day of man has come
The day of man is here
All nations do quiver and shake
All beings have cause to fear

But every day has its limits
Can last only so long
When it is with us it's good
When it is gone it's gone

Prepare for the future
The time to come
That when the future comes
We'll be able our race to run

PEOPLE WORRY ABOUT THE MIGHTY

People worry about the mighty
What makes them so?
Are they so different from us?
We would like to know

The mighty are beyond our reach
It's not for most of us
To know how to build
How to take nature's fuss

We can be mighty
In the right time and place
But we must be up to the test
We must our challenges face

But we must remember
The mighty are out there
Everyone sees what they do
Their every action people stare

They cannot hide from the people
Their private time has gone away
They may wish to hide from us
Not hear what people say

EVERYONE WISHES FOR PEACE

Everyone wishes for peace
They want it so
But the peace they want
Is peace only they can know

Can all know peace in time
That makes them want to live the day
their every want to hold
Their own way each and every day

The peace of God is the inner peace
That others cannot know
For the inner peace is ours
When the winds of adversity blow

ONE WISH

If you could have one wish
There is nothing to comment
One wish granted by all powers
For eternity you will enjoy it

What would this one wish be?
Not what comes to mind
Not what you desire now
Not for which you pine

A wish that is eternal
As good as it can be
For He who we need to please
Is the One who made the tree

WHAT WILL TOMORROW BRING

What will tomorrow bring?
What will be on that day?
Will we know what to do?
Will we know what to say?

The future we cannot know
A blank slate it appears to be
But when life writes upon the time
It becomes the present we see

We must so live in this world
That we may do the right
For if we live by doing wrong
We will lose the Holy Light

NEVER STOP LEARNING

Never stop learning
When you do, you're dead
The more you know
The less you have to dread

Discipline yourself
In body, mind and soul
If you do not
Life will take its toll

It's not either/or
Learning and living each day
It's both/and with
Great dividends to pay

WE MUST WAIT TO GROW

We must wait to grow
We think that is the way
If we do not prepare
It is the very devil we will pay

We wait to go to school
To pass every grade
So much to learn and know
It is this part of life that's made

We wait to get a job
A source of money to have
But to get real money
An education we must have

We wait to live our life
And as we sit and wait
Life passes us by
If we live in hate

But we must work
To make a better end
For when we get there
We find that life did just begin

ON WAITING

Waiting is a part of life
Something we do everyday
Some of us stand and stare
Others sit and play

Waiting can be tiresome
It takes our very soul
But we must prepare
Else life will take its toll

Waiting is not what we would do
If there were any other way
For we have better things
Than to throw our time away

AGAINST ALL ODDS

Against all odds
Humans have made it
From the claws of nature
To the traps we have set

We don't know how
Or why it is so
But gratitude is becoming
For those in the know

For nature is against us
Also our fellow men
But by divine providence
We live on the land

A BAGEL, A BAGEL

A bagel, a bagel
A 3 o'clock kagel
What makes the river swoon
It use to flow within its banks
Now it flows too soon

The rain came down
The falling would never stop
When it had filled
The river came over the top

The flood came and made us wet
Washed away all we had
But there is a new beginning
For which we should be glad

BREAK, BREAK, BREAK

Break, break, break
Upon life's future break
The waves of the future
Cannot the present take

The present is what we know
In terms of a past event
Through the tunnel of time
The future is never spent

But the present is not alone
Determined by what came before
It is in the present where we live
Made in the forges of yore

The past does the present make
As surely as we are here
But the future the present makes
For the future is very near

THINK OF THE FUTURE

Think of the future
It'll be better than the past
From now to forever
As long as it will last

Everything is a resource
To be used for our best
For we do truly live
In the age of the blest

But look to the morrow
It'll be here before we know
The evil we do today
Will make us shudder so

A SUDDEN MOVE

A sudden move
From where you are
Can change your life
Separate you by far

We all must move
From time to time
To keep our careers
In the pink, in the prime

But if the move we make
Are within our family's life
For when we move within there
It may cause internal strife

We do not like the new
That we do not know
But it is the future
That makes our spirit grow

PREPARE

Prepare, prepare
Prepare for the future
The land where we will live
Remember this axiom
"Expect others not to give"

The future we cannot see
Shrouded in the fog of the mind
But if we do not plan for the future
The future will not be kind

Prepare and plan
Plan and prepare
No matter what you think is fair
The future will be different
When we all get there

So what to do
What to say
Do good with what you have
For the future may take it away

A TETHER

A tether, a tatter, a trump
The future makes me jump
There's much I don't know
About the row I must hoe
That will give me a lump

When the future is here
Will we stand up and cheer?
To know what it brings
Whether a peasant or a king

We can never see beyond
The bend in the road of time
So let us live the best
That makes our life worthwhile

WHEN THE END HAS COME

When at last the end has come
Our soul departed, our body died
We cross that great chasm
We will be on the other side

Then our life will be an open book
Our deeds, our words, our thoughts
The bad as well as the good
The sum of all we have wrought

We will be judged by our Maker
Our soul weighed on that eternal scale
Rewarded by our Holy Father
His justice will never fail

So love and trust and live
That when life's race you've run
You will live in eternal glory
Under the Holy, Everlasting Son

WHEN I LOOK AT THE FUTURE

When I look at the future
Or at the past
I wonder if after I'm gone
Will anything I've done last

All things we do
Both small and great
Are left at death's door
For others to love or hate

Some things that endure
Things that last
Are things that will
Make the future, the past

THE FUTURE

What has happened in the past
Are things we cannot change
The bad and the good
Fall into a full range

Where we are now in life
Results from decisions made
By others and by ourselves
By the price that was paid

But where we are going
Is what we will now make
It is the future that belongs to us
It is the path we will take

THE FUTURE IS A QUESTION

The future is a question
A dark hole into which we peer
We don't know what it'll be
Until we get there

Look into the future
Determine what's there
If we knew where we were going
Life would be quite fair

But we don't know the promise
The future will hold
So we can but do our best
With opportunities we behold

A PLASTIC SHIP

A plastic ship
Upon a glass sea
A charcoal moon
In a celestial tree

The stroke of luck
The hole in one
Will the graces bring
When the future does come?

Do not be discouraged
From doing what is right
For from the fountain of truth
Will shine heaven's light

A FLASH OF LIGHT IN DARKNESS

A flash of light in darkness
A trick of the eye
It is as though darkness
Has filled the sky

But the flashes come from within
By imagination and born of a trick
It means that something can happen
Not necessarily that you're sick

Use your eyes
To see both bad and good
While you can see
Do the good you should

TIME IS A RIVER

Time is a river which flows to infinity
It comes from the past carrying us along
We cannot get off the river
For this is life's song

The beginning is in a dark past
From whence it comes
We can speculate the cause
By the way time runs

But we are given a little time
To live and work and love
This is the basis of our life
With faith from above

TIME

From the beginning of the beginning
To the end of the end
Life is a journey
Which good things doth send

We cannot know the end
Of what we say and do
We can only attempt
To make sure that it is kind and true

We walk the path of life
We walk it steady and true
Our responsibility for life
Is what we say and do

So make it what you would
This is all you can do
By the best you have
To those you love be ever true

GOALS

Life is a process of doing
Goals set and achieved
Often these are set by us
When we complete them we're relieved

To accomplish a goal in life
To finally succeed
Is such a great relief
When the goal has been achieved

Goals are the stuff of life
Making everyone bold
Completing them from our list
Making them as closed

There's winning and losing
There's how we play the game
Never let anyone tell you
The end is all the same

But work for the better
For what the future brings
Because if you do your best
It will cause the angels to sing

THE END OF TOMORROW

We walk the path of life
We go from day to day
We do not know the future
But we can find the way

There are paths we trod
As we go toward our goal
Always we look to the end
That sits upon our soul

There may never be a tomorrow
When we run so fast
For the decisions we make today
May not result in what will last

So let us not hurry through life
To those who don't value today
Because when you reach the end
It will make your lifetime pay

For tomorrow may never come
To those who do not value today
For the mistakes that you make
May bring a heavy cost to pay

If we do not plan as we go
But hurry past in life
When we get to the next thing
We may find our world full of strife

ST. IVES

As I was going to St. Ives
I met a man with seven wives
Why would a man have seven wives?
Supporting them would be a hard row to hoe

No man can support seven women
No matter how much his wealth
We should not bite off more than we can chew
We could make a different choice if we knew

So as we do our best
We think we are blest
But we must our secrets keep
If we would at night sleep

So be satisfied with what we have
To have enough to give with love
That we will be so remembered
When our soul is sent above

THE SHELL GATHERS

Along the beach the tide comes in
Along the beach the tide goes out
The incoming tide brings shells
The outgoing tide leaves shells

The shell gatherers come with the day
It is nature's bounty they seek
The early gatherers get the best
The later ones get the rest

The shell seekers come when they may
They know what they seek
Every hour of the day
Every day of the week

Some find the best shells
That is the gift of the sea
It is the gift of nature
To all, both you and me

Some shells are very rare
They are few and far between
But when we find them on the beach
They are something to behold when seen

So we go onto the beach
In the heat of the day
For those who gather shells
The beautiful shells will be their prey

ADVICE

When going through life
Advice is easy to give
If you receive such advice
Say "Thank you" if it helps you live

Sometimes advice is given
That some think is true
Ask yourself "Is there a basis for this"
The advice that they gave to you

Always receive advice
As a gift others have given
For if this is something that is important to you
It may be from you hidden

Then remember the proverb that applies
"If one person calls you an ass ignore it
If two people call you an ass
Get thee a saddle"

THE CHANGING FUTURE

For each of us there is a future
We can see as we look down the corridors of time
We can imagine how the future will be
What in the future will be mine

We expect the future to be more of today
Based on the world we now have
But when the future is the present
We will see what it will give

Things will change in many ways
From our current situation
We can hope it will be there
And not from our expectations

We must prepare for the future
Prepare for what we now see
But I will always be flexible
When the future covers me

WEALTH

When we think of a person with wealth
We think of someone with lots of things
They have whatever they want
It would make the multitude sing

There are many things that give us wealth
Things that money cannot buy
We may have enough of things to be content
At least we should try

What does a person need?
To be showered in wealth?
A good, loving home and family
Most importantly, good health

THE WISHING TREE

When I was a child
I wanted a tree
Whose fruit would come
To be just for me

I'd wish for many things
For gold and candy and cars
But finding a wishing tree
Was just not in my stars

Now I am a man
I have come to be me
But still I'd like to have
My very own wishing tree

SOME SURFACES

Some surfaces are flat
Some are round
Some set us in motion
Some get us down

As with surfaces
So it is with life
Sometimes life is stable
Sometimes filled with strife

Whatever the outcome
Often depends on us
Whether we accept the facts
Or raise a fuss

The secret of life
Is not just what we do
But to know the situation
It all depends on you

GEOMETRY

Geometry is the study of shapes
The configuration of lines
It looks at similar arrangements
That changes not over time

But there are shapes in life
That are not on paper drawn
They are here for us
Although the reason does not on us dawn

There are restraints in our work
In our social life also
We are expected
These lines to know

When we cross these lines
Violate some social rule
We will be given the cold shoulder
By those who think us a fool

PAPER PLANES

Paper planes
And toy trains
Make a child's fanciful world
Jet planes
Freight trains
Make an adult's real world

We all pretend
To know the end
That we would like to achieve
But in the end
It is as we begin
Fanciful is what we believe

So we can make the world as we would
We do the best we could
To act as we know we will
For the planes
And the trains
Are ours to fit our bill

CLIMB THE TALLEST MOUNTAIN

Climb the tallest mountain
Cross the deep blue sea
This is the way we go
To have a blessing from Thee

There is no other way
That we may cross and see
From beginning to the end
Is what it will forever be

No one knows the way of men
Who seeks the holy end
But as we go out
Life's journey to begin

For as the journey of life
From birth until eternity begins
We think about the way of life
Until we get to the end

MEET THE AUTHOR

Richard Gold was born in Bartow, Florida and attended college and worked for the Government for 40 years. He has been a Christian and writing poems for as long. Gold is now retired which gives him the time necessary to continue to write. Gold lives in Indian Head, Maryland with Penny, his artistically talented wife.

www.ingramcontent.com/pod-product-compliance
Lightning Source LLC
Chambersburg PA
CBHW031613040426
42452CB00006B/498